CENTRAL AMERICA
TODAY

Costa Rica

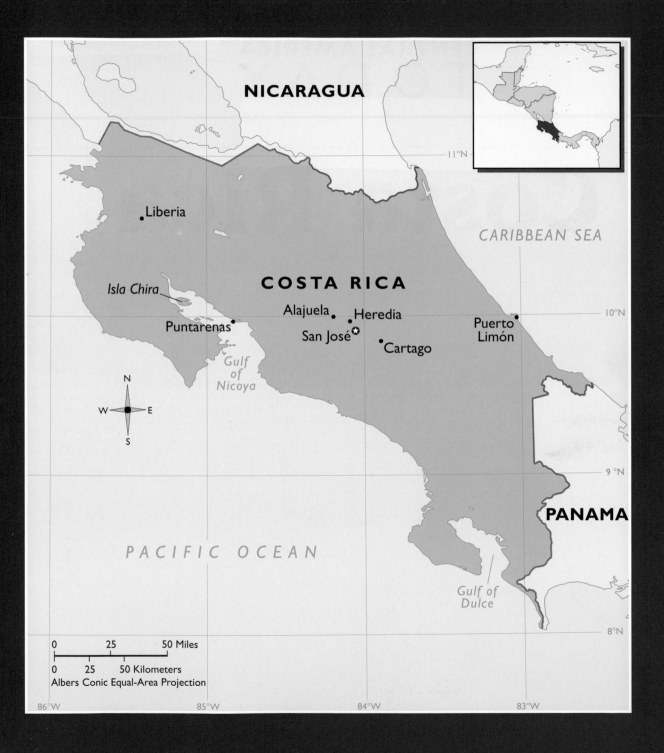

CENTRAL AMERICA
TODAY

Costa Rica

Charles J. Shields

Mason Crest Publishers
Philadelphia

Produced by OTTN Publishing, Stockton, N.J.

Mason Crest Publishers
370 Reed Road
Broomall PA 19008
www.masoncrest.com

Printed and bound in Malaysia.

CPISA compliance information: Batch#10310-CA3.
For further information, contact Mason Crest Publishers at 610-543-6200.

 3 5 7 9 8 6 4

Library of Congress Cataloging-in-Publication Data

Shields, Charles J., 1951-
   Costa Rica / Charles J. Shields.
        p. cm. —   (Central America today)
   Includes index.
   ISBN 978-1-4222-0646-1 (hardcover) — ISBN 978-1-4222-0713-0 (pbk.)
   1. Costa Rica—Juvenile literature. [1. Costa Rica.] I. Title.
   F1544.S55 2008
   972.86—dc22
                                      2008031993

CENTRAL AMERICA
TODAY

Belize
Central America: Facts and Figures
Costa Rica
El Salvador

Guatemala
Honduras
Nicaragua
Panama

Discovering Central America

James D. Henderson

CENTRAL AMERICA is a beautiful part of the world, filled with generous and friendly people. It is also a region steeped in history, one of the first areas of the New World explored by Christopher Columbus. Central America is both close to the United States and strategically important to it. For nearly a century ships of the U.S. and the world have made good use of the Panama Canal. And for longer than that breakfast tables have been graced by the bananas and other tropical fruits that Central America produces in abundance.

Central America is closer to North America and other peoples of the world with each passing day. Globalized trade brings the region's products to world markets as never before. And there is promise that trade agreements will soon unite all nations of the Americas in a great common market. Meanwhile improved road and air links make it easy for visitors to reach Middle America. Central America's tropical flora and fauna are ever more accessible to foreign visitors having an interest in eco-tourism. Other visitors are drawn to the region's dazzling Pacific Ocean beaches, jewel-like scenery, and bustling towns and cities. And everywhere Central America's wonderful and varied peoples are outgoing and welcoming to foreign visitors.

These eight books are intended to provide complete, up-to-date information on the five countries historians call Central America (Guatemala, El Salvador, Honduras, Nicaragua, Costa Rica), as well as on Panama (technically part of South America) and Belize (technically part of North America). Each volume contains chapters on the land, history, economy, people, and cultures of the countries treated. And each country study is written in an engaging style, employing a vocabulary appropriate to young students.

A coffee plantation in Costa Rica.

All volumes contain colorful illustrations, maps, and up-to-date boxed information of a statistical character, and each is accompanied by a chronology, a glossary, a bibliography, selected Internet resources, and an index. Students and teachers alike will welcome the many suggestions for individual and class projects and reports contained in each country study, and they will want to prepare the tasty traditional dishes described in each volume's recipe section.

This eight-book series is a timely and useful addition to the literature on Central America. It is designed not just to inform, but also to engage school-aged readers with this important and fascinating part of the Americas.

Let me introduce this series as author Charles J. Shields begins each volume: *¡Hola!* You are discovering Central America!

Costa Rica is a country with many volcanoes, such as Arenal (opposite). There are more than 200 volcanic formations in Costa Rica, some of which date as far back as 65 million years. Seven of Central America's 42 active volcanoes are in Costa Rica, as well as 60 dormant or extinct volcanoes. (Right) A horse and rider on the coast at Playa Tamarindo.

1 A Tropical Land of Mountains, Beaches, and Forests

¡HOLA! ARE YOU DISCOVERING Costa Rica? It is beautiful there! Costa Rica has tall mountains, white beaches, plunging waterfalls, tropical islands, and cool, green jungles where monkeys will lope right up to within camera range. Costa Ricans are very friendly, too. Men call themselves *ticos*, and women are *ticas*. If someone asks you, "*¿Cómo está usted?*" ("How are you?"), just reply "*¡Tota bien!*", which means "Absolutely great!"

Costa Rica: Small but Diverse

At 19,730 square miles (51,100 square kilometers), Costa Rica is the second-smallest Central American nation after El Salvador. It is barely bigger than the state of New Hampshire. At its narrowest point, in the south, only 74 miles (119 kilometers) separate the Caribbean from the Pacific—just a five-hour drive. At its broadest point, Costa Rica is only 175 miles (280 kilometers) wide. On the eastern seaboard, barely 100 miles (160 kilometers) separate the Nicaraguan and Panamanian borders. The Pacific coast is longer, but it is still only 300 miles (480 kilometers) from the northernmost tip to the Panamanian border in the south.

Lying between 8° and 11° north of the equator, Costa Rica is located entirely within the tropics. But vast differences in elevation create more

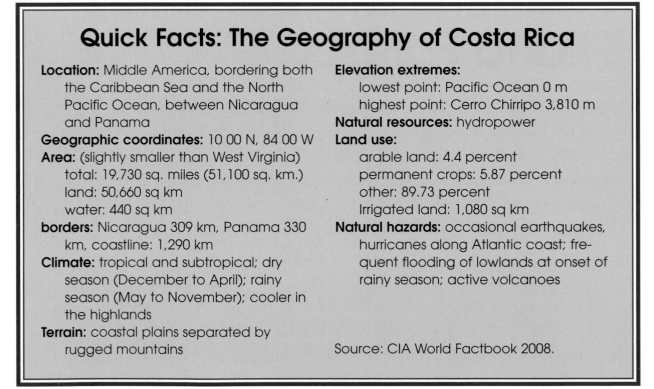

Quick Facts: The Geography of Costa Rica

Location: Middle America, bordering both the Caribbean Sea and the North Pacific Ocean, between Nicaragua and Panama

Geographic coordinates: 10 00 N, 84 00 W

Area: (slightly smaller than West Virginia)
total: 19,730 sq. miles (51,100 sq. km.)
land: 50,660 sq km
water: 440 sq km

borders: Nicaragua 309 km, Panama 330 km, coastline: 1,290 km

Climate: tropical and subtropical; dry season (December to April); rainy season (May to November); cooler in the highlands

Terrain: coastal plains separated by rugged mountains

Elevation extremes:
lowest point: Pacific Ocean 0 m
highest point: Cerro Chirripo 3,810 m

Natural resources: hydropower

Land use:
arable land: 4.4 percent
permanent crops: 5.87 percent
other: 89.73 percent
Irrigated land: 1,080 sq km

Natural hazards: occasional earthquakes, hurricanes along Atlantic coast; frequent flooding of lowlands at onset of rainy season; active volcanoes

Source: CIA World Factbook 2008.

than a dozen distinct climatic zones. Even ice and snow aren't unknown in cooler months atop the highest mountains.

In fact, Costa Rica is one of the few places in the world where the forces of nature are constantly overlapping and even clashing. A dozen different climatic patterns exist side-by-side. Far beneath the ground, gigantic *tectonic* plates—the Cocos and Caribbean plates—barge into one another, triggering earthquakes and sometimes volcanic eruptions. In addition, the *flora* and *fauna* of both North and South America meet in Costa Rica, adding even more eye-pleasing variety to the diversity of terrain and weather that makes Costa Rica special.

Microclimates for Weather

Although Costa Rica is located within the tropics, it has about a dozen tiny climatic zones, or *microclimates*. Thus, it is hard to speak broadly about temperature and rainfall in Costa Rica. In general, the coastal regions are hotter than the central valley. For instance, it is usually around 72° F (22° C) in the Central Valley, 82° F (28° C) on the Atlantic coast, and 89° F (31.5° C) on the Pacific coast. The differences depend mainly on elevation. The most extreme daily temperature changes occur during the dry season, when clear skies at night allow maximum heat loss. In the wet season, nights are generally warmer, as clouds trap the heat from the day.

Most regions have a dry season (December through April), and a rainy season, or Green Season, as it's called locally (May through November). The Green Season brings daily afternoon rains to the country. Annual rainfall averages 100 inches nationwide, with some mountainous regions getting as much as 25 feet on exposed eastern slopes! Abundant rain supplies water for agriculture, as well as feeding hundreds of rivers and dozens of spectacular waterfalls.

A Backbone of Mountains

Costa Rica has four distinct *cordilleras*, or mountain ranges—Guanacaste and Tilaran in the north, Central and Talamanca in the south—that, together, run like a rugged backbone from northwest to southeast through the landscape. The *cordilleras* divide the country into three land regions: the Central Highlands, the Caribbean Lowlands, and the Pacific Coastal Strip.

The Central Highlands consist of two large areas of fertile farmland—the Meseta Central (Central Plateau) and the Valle del General (Valley of the General). Both are surrounded by the steep sides of the *cordilleras*. The Meseta Central is the country's heartland, where about 60 percent of Costa Ricans live. The Meseta Central's rich volcanic soil and favorable climate also make it the country's chief coffee-growing region. The Valle del General lies to the southeast, an agricultural region of hills and plains.

White- and black-sand beaches edge Costa Rica's second and third regions, the Caribbean Lowlands and the Pacific Coastal Strip. On the east coast, thick bands of swampy tropical jungle twist through the Caribbean Lowlands. On the west coast, mountains come closer to the ocean than on the Caribbean side, sometimes creating a coastal plain just a few miles wide with spectacular beaches. The Pacific Coastal Strip is deeply indented with multiple bays, inlets, and two large gulfs: the Gulf of Nicoya in the north and Golfo Dulce in the south. The climate of the Pacific Coastal Strip is ideal for growing bananas.

Along Costa Rica's east coast, there are thick tropical rainforests. These jungle regions provide homes for hundreds of different species of animals.

Off the Pacific coast, in the Gulf of Nicoya, are most of Costa Rica's islands. Their total land area is only about 40 square miles. The largest is 17-mile-square Chira at the upper end of the gulf, the only one with electricity, medical services, and schools to support a permanent population of 2,000. Most of Chira's residents fish or farm for a living. Costa Rica's national parks system protects a handful of the other islands, several of which serve as habitats for sea birds.

Costa Rica's *cordilleras* are also one of the most active volcanic regions on earth. Volcanologists have identified over 200 volcanic formations in Costa Rica, dating as far back as 65 million years. Some of the volcanoes rise as graceful cones to a single crater. Others are squat, weather-beaten mountains whose tops collapsed into huge depressions, called *calderas*, the Spanish word for cauldron. A third kind has smooth outlines with rounded tops pockmarked by tiny craters, such as those on Cocos Island.

Costa Rica's active volcanoes are young—formed within the last two million years—such as Arenal, Poás, Irazú, and Turrialba. Arenal stands alone on the plain, a classic cone against the sky. Poás's main crater is more than a mile across and 1,000 feet deep with an acid lake in its center. Irazú's peak looks like the surface of the moon—rocky and lifeless. Turrialba, which resembles Irazú, is a wilderness.

Costa Rica also experiences earth **tremors** and small earthquakes occasionally. During one two-month period in 1989, **seismologists** recorded more than 16,000 tremors in Costa Rica. Most, however, were not felt by

There are hundreds of species of birds and animals that live only in Costa Rica. Among them are the coppery-headed emerald hummingbird, shown here getting something to eat in the rain forest.

anyone. The reason for the tremors and quakes is that Costa Rica lies at the place where the Pacific's Cocos Plate—a piece of the earth's crust some 3,188 miles (510 km) wide—meets another plate under the Caribbean. The two are rubbing, jostling and shoving each other as the Cocos Plate moves east at a rate of about four inches a year. The last major quake hit on November 20, 2004, measuring 6.4 on the *Richter scale*.

A Bio-Geographical Land Bridge

Costa Rica means "rich coast," and preserving its rich natural resources is a high priority. The land that is Costa Rica was thrust up from the ocean floor only several million years ago. At different times, volcanoes and earthquakes transformed it into an isthmus, a peninsula, and even an *archipelago*. The rich volcanic soil supports dense and diverse forests and jungles—homes to monkeys, butterflies, birds, and reptiles. Thousands of species of plants and animals have arrived over the ages, blended, and flourished on this bio-geographical land bridge between the North and South American continents. In fact, many scientists claim that despite its small size, Costa Rica has more species than any other land habitat in the world.

Costa Rica has approximately 200 species of mammals, 160 of amphibians, 200 of reptiles, 1,000 of butterflies, and 850 of birds—more species of birds than in the entire North American continent. Scientists have also identified over 10,000 species of higher plants, or 4 percent of the earth's known total. The National Parks and Forestry Services has nearly 3 million acres, or 25 percent of Costa Rica's national territory, under protection.

(Opposite) A July 1953 rally for Jose Figueres, the popular candidate of Costa Rica's National Liberation Party. The day after this photograph was taken in San Jose, Figueres was elected president of the country. (Right) Oscar Arias Sánchez addresses journalists in Brazil, July 2008. Arias became president of Costa Rica for the second time in 2006.

2 The History of Costa Rica Follows a Remarkable Course

NATIVE AMERICAN communities dotted the landscape of present-day Costa Rica at least 10,000 years before Christopher Columbus arrived on the Pacific coast of the country in 1502. High mountains and swampy lowlands tended to isolate the ancient tribes living here from the Incas and Mayas of Peru and Mexico. But archeological digs at Guayabo, Costa Rica, have unearthed streets, *aqueducts*, and *causeways*, suggesting a link with the great Indian civilizations of Central and South America.

Some of the prehistoric tribes of Costa Rica, such as the Caribs on the Caribbean and the Borucas in the southwest, were *semi-nomadic* hunters and fishers who raised yucca and squash, chewed coca, and lived in shared village huts surrounded by fortified log fences. The female-led Chibchas

17

had an extensive slave system and were artistic goldsmiths.

The largest tribe of the region, the Chorotegas, was probably the most accomplished. Their name means "fleeing people," and they came from southern Mexico during the 14th century. A warlike people, with slaves, high priests, and nobles, the Chorotegas built towns and plazas. Their large-scale agriculture produced beans, corn, squash, and gourds. In the arts, they wrote stories on deerskin parchment and crafted ceramics and jade figures.

The Coming of the Europeans

When Columbus arrived near present-day Puerto Limón on September 18, 1502, during his fourth and last voyage to the Americas, perhaps only 20,000 Native Americans lived in the region. The local people greeted him in a friendly fashion, sending out two girls ages 8 and 14. Columbus's son, Ferdinand, recorded, "The girls . . . always looked cheerful and modest." The Europeans gave them gifts. Then, adult Indian dignitaries appeared wearing gold, which they gave to Columbus. "I saw more signs of gold in the first two days than I saw in Española during four years," he noted in his journal. He called the region La Huerta (The Garden). But his ship was becoming unseaworthy, and after 17 days, Columbus was forced to leave for Spain, never to return.

Spaniards who followed Columbus received gifts of gold, too. By 1539, the territory between Panama and Nicaragua had become officially known as Costa Rica—"the rich coast." European adventurers and explorers tried to penetrate the interior in hopes of finding even more treasure. Instead, they slogged through swamps, suffered from disease, and fought off the attacks of angered tribes. In 1562, Spain sent Juan Vásquez de Coronado to Costa Rica to act as governor. Europeans and natives did not live close together, however. Most Native Americans fled the Spanish settlement areas because European diseases such as ophthalmia, smallpox, and tuberculosis had ravaged their tribes. Many of the natives died from these diseases in the decades after the Spanish arrived. The European settlements fared poorly, also. The Spaniards were unable to put the native people to work for them, unlike in other areas of Central and South America, so they were forced to to scratch out farms alone.

By the early 1800s, centuries-long colonial poverty in Costa Rica led Governor Tomás de Acosta to observe that life had changed little since ancient Indians farmed the land. Then, in 1821, Guatemala proclaimed independence from Spain for all of Central America. Costa Rica, though it had never previously tried to rebel against Spain, held its first elections that same year. The new government started building roads and schools and encouraging new businesses. In 1848, Costa Rica declared itself a free and independent republic.

Independence and Progress

Strangely, the first real challenge to Costa Rica's independence came at the hands of an American lawyer, doctor,

Did You Know?

- Costa Rica is a democratic republic. The capital is San José.
- Independence Day is celebrated September 15. Costa Rica declared its independence from Spain on that date in 1821. It declared itself a free and independent republic in 1848.
- The current constitution was ratified on November 7, 1949.

and soldier of fortune from Tennessee named William Walker. Walker dreamed of conquering all of Central America and joining the countries together as part of a larger "Confederacy of Southern American States." After serving as a hired commander-in-chief of Nicaragua's army to put down a rebellion, Walker stepped in as Nicaragua's unelected president. He next set his sights on Costa Rica and dispatched a small army to invade it.

Costa Rica did not have a strong national identity, but rumors of being enslaved by *mercenaries* inspired a spirited defense. A poorly equipped force of several thousand Costa Ricans repelled Walker's men in March 1856, and sent them fleeing back into Nicaragua. A bloody second battle in April ended in Costa Rican victory when two young men—Juan Santamaría, a Costa Rican, and a second volunteer, a Nicaraguan—accepted a suicide mission to set fire to the enemy's fort. Walker's forces retreated, and Santamaría became Costa Rica's first and only war hero.

The invasion scare set off a period of military rule. The coffee barons—wealthy coffee plantation owners—had counted on the military to support them in the 1860s. In 1870, however, General Tomás Guardia overthrew the government and ruled with an iron hand for 12 years.

Guardia was a *caudillo*, a charismatic authoritarian leader. Unlike most dictators, however, he was a forward-looking thinker. He abolished capital punishment; curbed

William Walker (1824–1860) was an American, but he became president of Nicaragua in 1856. One of his first acts was an invasion of Costa Rica that failed.

the power of the coffee barons and the military; used taxes to build roads and public buildings; contracted with an American, Minor Keith, to build a railroad through the rugged landscape from the capital San José to the Caribbean; and revised the constitution to provide free, mandatory "primary education for both sexes." In essence, he laid the foundation for a modern Costa Rica. His influence could be seen in the election of 1889, when mass demonstrations forced President Bernardo Soto to resign because he claimed reelection in spite of the popular vote.

> ### Did You Know?
>
> - The social security system was established in 1941 and provides services to over 80 percent of the population.
> - Approximately 22.1 percent of Costa Rica's national budget is used for public health matters.
> - There are 30 hospitals and 116 clinics in Costa Rica. They provide a total of over 7,000 beds in a network of public and private institutions.

Progress toward democracy continued after 1889 (women and blacks, however, were still excluded from voting), except for when in 1917, Federico Tinoco seized the presidency. After political protest forced him to resign two years later, Costa Rica resumed its course in the direction of democracy and social reform.

Civil War and Democratic Reforms

The next important era in Costa Rican political history began with the election of Dr. Rafael Angel Calderón Guardia in 1940. A physician with a social conscience, Calderón focused on the poor. During his term as president from 1940–44, he pushed through policies of land reform that favored poor farmers, passed a minimum wage law, and put in place a system of

Costa Rican troops, called Mariachis, march through a town during Costa Rica's 1948 civil war. The 40-day war cost the lives of 2,000 people, most of them civilians.

taxation weighted against the rich. But Calderón's party refused to step down after losing the 1948 election. Ten days later, civil war erupted.

The anti-Calderón forces were led by José María (Don Pepe) Figueres Ferrer, a 42-year-old coffee farmer, engineer, economist, and philosopher exiled to Mexico in 1942 for denouncing Calderón. Supported by the governments of Guatemala and Cuba, Don Pepe's rebels captured the cities of Cartago and Puerto Limón and were about to pounce on San José when Calderón yielded. Don Pepe then returned the reins of power to Otilio Ulate, the actual winner of the 1948 election—a man not even of Don Pepe's own party.

Costa Ricans later rewarded Figueres with two terms as president, in 1953–57 and 1970–74. For the next two decades, Don Pepe dominated politics in Costa Rica. He continued the reforms introduced by Calderón, and introduced many of his own, as well. Despite support from Cuba during the civil war, he banned the Communist Party; gave women the vote and granted full citizenship to blacks; established a term limit for presidents; turned banks and insurance companies over to government control; and abolished the military. Since then, Costa Rica has been widely known as the "country without an army." Don Pepe died in 1990 a national hero.

In 1983, in response to nearby civil wars in Central America, Costa Rica issued a proclamation of neutrality. In 1986, Costa Ricans elected as their president a young sociologist and lawyer, Oscar Arias Sánchez, who promised to work for peace. As a result of his efforts, five Central American presidents signed his peace plan in Guatemala City in 1987, for which he received the Nobel Peace Prize that year.

In 1990, Rafael Angel Calderón Fournier, son of the reformer elected in 1940, won a narrow victory with 51 percent of the vote. Calderón was inaugurated 50 years to the day after Costa Rica named his father president. For most of his term in office, he devoted his energies to restoring Costa Rica's economic health, which had been battered by a difficult period in the 1980s. His policies helped retire the country's heavy national debt.

Oscar Arias Sánchez, the president of Costa Rica from 1986 to 1990, won the 1987 Nobel Peace Prize for his program for peace in Central America. He was re-elected president in 2006.

Then, by a further coincidence of history, in 1994, Calderón, whose father had been ousted by Don Pepe Figueres in 1948, lost his reelection bid to Don Pepe's son, José María Figueres-Olsen, a graduate of West Point and Harvard. During his four-year term, Figueres's theme was "sustainable development." He promoted information technology and investment in Costa Rica by high-tech firms.

Costa Rica holds a unique place in the history of Central America. From its days as a colony of Spain to its current status as a burgeoning democracy with *progressive* policies, Costa Rica has steered a remarkable course, unmarred by major wars or crippling social upheaval.

(Opposite) Bananas are being loaded onto trucks and donkeys near the town of Golfito, circa 1950. Although farm products such as bananas, coffee, and cattle are still a large part of Costa Rica's economy, industry and tourism have increased since the 1990s. This has led to construction of new facilities, such as the Tambor Tropical Hotel (right).

3 A Changing Economy

COSTA RICA'S MAIN economic resources are its fertile land and regular rainfall, its well-educated population, and its location, which provides access to North and South American markets and ocean access to Europe and Asia. In addition, its beautiful beaches and government-protected preserves are attracting a fast-growing number of tourists to Costa Rica.

Costa Rica's *economy* used to rely on agriculture. Farmers primarily raised bananas and coffee. Since the 1990s, though, income from manufacturing and industry has contributed more to Costa Rica's economy than agriculture. Intel Corporation, for example, employs nearly 2,000 people at its $300 million microprocessor plant; and Proctor & Gamble has located its administrative center for the Western Hemisphere in Costa Rica. Tourism is

25

also booming. More than half of all new *investment* in Costa Rica is related to tourism in the form of new hotels, restaurants, and recreation areas. In the last ten years or so, tourism has become Costa Rica's leading source of income.

Natural Beauty Draws Eco-Tourists

In May 1990, the Costa Rican government appointed its first tourism minister to the president's cabinet to help plan for the rapidly increasing number of tourists—mostly from the United States—who visit the country. The number of tourists rose, for example, from 780,000 to over 1 million between 1996 and 1999. Two international airports connect foreign visitors to local airline flights, making travel to most regions in Costa Rica easy. The Pan American Highway links all of Costa Rica's provincial capitals, except

Today, more than a million people visit Costa Rica each year, making tourism the country's top source of revenue. Many people who come to Costa Rica are drawn by its natural beauty. These whitewater rafters are visiting Cocos Island.

Puerto Limón. The government is also improving roads to popular destinations, such as Cahuita, Flamingo, Monteverde, Quepos, Sámara, Tamarindo, and Tambor. In major cities and towns, buses and taxis are inexpensive and widely used.

Many visitors come to Costa Rica as "eco-tourists." **Eco-tourism** means responsible travel that contributes to conserving natural environments and puts money into the hands of the local people. Costa Rica's mountains and volcanoes, for instance, provide lakes and rivers for fishing, swimming, and boating; white-water rapids for exciting rafting and kayaking; and wilderness preserves for horseback riding, hiking, camping and mountain biking. A 1986 study by the Costa Rican Tourism Institute found that 87 percent of tourists surveyed said natural beauty was one of their main reasons for visiting Costa Rica; 36 percent specifically mentioned eco-tourism.

The government of Costa Rica has tried to manage the boom in eco-tourism without damaging the environment that people come to see. In 1977, the country adopted the Maritime Terrestrial Zone Law, which declares the country's entire coastline to be public property and restricts construction along the shore. Businesses that offer tours to natural areas are supposed to respect the Code of Environmental **Ethics** for Nature Travel established by Tsuli/Tsuli—the Costa Rican chapter of the National

Did You Know?

- Costa Rica's flag has five horizontal bands of blue (top), white, red (double width), white, and blue, with the coat of arms in a white disk on the hoist side of the red band.
- The national bird is the yigüirro, a peaceful bird that sings at the start of the rainy season.
- The national flower is the guaria morada, an orchid that grows everywhere.
- The national tree is the guanacaste, a native tree whose name means "curled ear" because that is what its leaves look like.

Audubon Society. In October 1991, Costa Rica was chosen as one of three winners of the first environmental award presented by the American Society of Travel Agents (ASTA) and *Smithsonian Magazine*. The award recognizes a "company, individual, or country for achievements in conservation and environmentalism."

The National Parks Service in Costa Rica is in charge of managing 20 national parks, eight biological reserves, and Guayabo National Monument—Costa Rica's most important archaeological site, with ruins dating back to around A.D. 300. The Forestry Department and National Wildlife Directorate maintains 26 protected zones, as well as forest reserves and animal sanctuaries for such creatures as the two- and three-toed sloth and the endangered squirrel monkey.

On the other hand, some critics of the soaring tourist industry in Costa Rica view with dismay the rise of "megaresorts," or enormous complexes of hotels and recreation areas. In Costa Rica's Gulf of Papagayo, for example, 6,000 tourists can stay in 2,000 rooms, 50 luxury villas, 400 family villas, and 700 apartments at the largest "leisure city" in Central America. Already, more than half of Costa Rica's workers are in *service industries*. For the sake of creating additional jobs, the government has made a goal of competing for tourists with popular vacation places in Mexico and the Caribbean. The shoreline of Costa Rica offers 1,800 beaches. Not all of them are safe, however, because of dangerous tides and undertows.

A Greater Demand for Goods

Manufacturing employs about a fifth of the *labor force* and is growing

Quick Facts: The Economy of Costa Rica

Inflation: 9.4 percent

Per capita income: $10,300

Natural resources: Hydroelectric power

Industry (29.4 percent of GDP*): microprocessors, food processing, medical equipment, textiles and clothing, construction materials, fertilizer, plastic products

Agriculture (8.6 percent of GDP): bananas, pineapples, coffee, melons, ornamental plants, sugar, corn, rice, beans, potatoes, beef, timber

Services (62.1 percent of GDP): Hotels, restaurants, tourist services, banks, and insurance

Foreign trade: Exports—$9.2 billion: bananas, pineapples, coffee, melons, ornamental plants, sugar, seafood, electronic components, medical components

Major markets (Imports 2006)
United States: 40.1 percent
Venezuela: 5.7 percent
Mexico: 5.7 percent
Japan: 5.3 percent
China: 5.1 percent
Brazil: 4.6 percent
Other: 33.5 percent

Currency exchange rate (August 2008): 551.815 colónes = US $1.

* GDP or gross domestic product—the total value of goods and services produced in a year. All figures are 2007 estimates, unless otherwise noted. Sources: CIA World Factbook 2008, Bloomberg.com

rapidly. Rising income among Costa Ricans has led to more purchasing power and a greater demand for goods. Manufacturing and industry in Costa Rica, however, is still rather limited. Local industrial raw materials are restricted to producing agricultural products, such as fertilizer, construction materials, and a small output of ores (Costa Rica has small deposits of bauxite and manganese). For export to other countries, though, Costa Rica offers electronic components, aluminum processing, textiles and clothing, small appliances, food processing, soap, cosmetics, and plastic products.

Costa Rica is expanding its economic and trade ties with other countries. In 1995, it signed a free trade agreement with Mexico removing tariffs on 8,000 goods. Exports that year increased 16 percent. In 2007, Costa Rica became part of the North American Free Trade Agreement (NAFTA), giving it greater access to markets in the United States.

A favorable sign for the growth of manufacturing and industry in Costa Rica is that the mountainous landscape and abundant rainfall creates rivers as energy sources. A system of a dozen *hydroelectric* and one *geothermal* plant provides plenty of electricity. (Electrical service is the same as in the United States: 120V, 60Hz). In fact, Costa Rica exports electricity to Nicaragua and may become a major energy provider for Central America. The reason Costa Rica can afford to export energy is that the mild climate makes heating or cooling unnecessary, even in the highland cities and towns where approximately 90 percent of the population lives.

From Coffee to Cattle

Farming and ranching employ about one-fourth of Costa Rica's workers. In the 19th and early 20th centuries, it was said that "coffee is king" in Costa Rica. Growing bananas was a close second. Since then, Costa Rican agriculture has branched out to include beef cattle, cacao (seeds used to make chocolate), corn, rice, and sugar cane, which together rank as the chief products. Oranges, beans, and potatoes, in addition to other fruits and vegetables, are important crops, too. Farmers also grow cut flowers. Acres of clear plastic in warmer areas protect fields of carnations and chrysanthemums. Lately, farmers are trying new crops for export, such as cassava (used in starches, tapioca, and livestock feeds), papaya, camote (sweet potato), melons, strawberries, chayote (vegetable pear), eggplant, curraré (plantain bananas), pimento, and macadamia nuts.

Farms and ranches can be seen everywhere in Costa Rica, even on the steepest slopes. About 12 percent of the land grows crops; 45 percent is given to pasture; and 27 percent is left forested. Vast coffee plantations roll across the misty Meseta Central and southern highlands, which yield some of the world's best coffee beans. In the Caribbean lowlands, plantations of slender banana trees produce approximately 50 million boxes of bananas a year, making Costa Rica the second biggest exporter of bananas in the world, even after a long workers' strike in 1985 in which United Fruit closed its banana-producing operations in southwestern Costa Rica. Today, many of those banana plantations have been turned over to growing African palms, which are used to produce things like cooking oil, margarine, and soap.

(Top) Workers clean bananas at the Chiquita plantation in Cahuita. Costa Rica remains the second-largest exporter of bananas in the world. (Bottom) A sugar mill in Turialba.

Of concern to environmentalists is the impact of cattle ranching on Costa Rica. Seventy percent of agricultural land is given to cattle pasture. Although beef shipments make up only about 9 percent of Costa Rica's export earnings, the land used to pasture herds of humpbacked zebu, Charolais, and Hereford cattle has been stripped bare of timber, causing floods in the Pacific lowlands.

Economic Forecast: Improving

Costa Ricans have suffered a bumpy economic ride over the past 15 years, although overall, there are signs that income levels will continue to rise and that they will enjoy a higher standard of living.

During the 1960s and 1970s, Costa Rica established a welfare state, providing health care and social service benefits to its population, which placed a severe financial strain on the government. In addition, many workers found employment with government offices, which added to the strain. Even today, the government pays the salaries of approximately 25 percent of the population, or one in four employed people.

Then, in the late 1970s and early 1980s, coffee prices fell and oil prices rose. The government borrowed heavily to meet its debts. *Inflation* reached 100 percent. By 1991, 35 percent of Costa

Did You Know?

- The government of Costa Rica currently spends about 21.4 percent of the national budget on education.
- Seventy percent of secondary education is provided by public schools.
- There are 3,879 educational centers, where more than 780,000 students are taught, including 60,000 university-level students.
- Ninety-six percent of the population has at least basic reading and writing skills.

Ricans were living below the poverty line. The United States and the International Monetary Fund (IMF) stepped in with a massive aid program that covered more than one-third of the Costa Rican's government budget. Only Israel received more per person from the United States in foreign aid. In return, Costa Rica agreed to side with the United States' aims in supporting a rebellion in Nicaragua.

Since then, government measures to cut back on spending have reduced the amount of poverty in Costa Rica. Economic growth has risen from -0.9 percent in 1996, to 4 percent in 1997, 6 percent in 1998, and 7 percent in 1999. Inflation, which was 22.5 percent in 1995, dropped to 11 percent in 1999, and is now 9.3 percent (2008).

Today, the average per-person income in Costa Rica is the equivalent of about $13,500. Costa Rica has an average of about one automobile for every 27 people. Most Costa Rican families own a radio. The country has about one television set for every six people. Eighty percent of the population has access to telephone services, which rank among the best in Latin America.

An exceptional part of Costa Rica is its health care services. In a United Nations study conducted in the 1980s, Costa Rica's medical system was first in Latin America and among the 20 best in the world. Figures from the World Health Organization's 1995 *World Health Report* place Costa Rica third in life expectancy in the world, behind Japan and France, but ahead of Great Britain and the United States. Many visitors to Costa Rica needing medical care are surprised to find world-class hospitals that offer services at modest prices, chiefly owing to the government's strong commitment to fund the health care system.

(Opposite) A group of children look at a display showing a map of Costa Rica in the Childrens Museum in San José. The museum was once a prison. (Right) in this photo taken in 1955, a group of Costa Ricans gather in a street cafe. The behavior and conversation of most residents of Costa Rica stems from *quedar bien*, a desire to leave a good impression.

4 "We Are All *Hermanitos*"

THE THREE MILLION Costa Ricans that currently constitute the population are the most racially alike of any Central Americans. They are 94 percent *mestizos* (of mixed white and Native American descent); three percent black; one percent Native American; one percent Chinese; and one percent belonging to other racial groups. The lighter complexion of Old World settlers can be seen everywhere. In fact "whiteness," and the lack of a strong surviving Indian culture, creates part of Costa Ricans' sense of national identity. They call themselves *ticos*, which probably comes from a saying in Spanish colonial days, "We are all *hermanitos* (little brothers)."

Ticos identify themselves first as Costa Ricans, and second as Central or Latin Americans. Each year at 6:00 P.M. on September 14—the eve of

35

Independence Day—Costa Ricans stop what they're doing and sing the national anthem. Peace, democracy, and personal liberty are cherished, and the people are proud of their steady progress toward these ideals over the last two centuries. Having no army, they tend to be suspicious of militaries, even protesting in the newspapers when the police receive more up-to-date weapons. Historically, *ticos* are proud of their ties to Spain, which they express first of all through their language—speaking correct Spanish is important—and second, through their manners and attitudes.

Overall, fairness and equality are important to Costa Ricans. Most say their country is a "classless democracy." They believe that with hard work and education, practically anyone can move up in their society, regardless

Quick Facts: The People of Costa Rica

Population: 4,195,914

Ethnic groups: 94 percent white/mestizo; 3 percent black; 1 percent Native American; 1 percent Chinese; 1 percent other.

Age structure:
0–14 years: 27.2 percent
15–64 years: 66.8 percent
65 years and over: 6 percent

Population growth rate: 1.39 percent

Birth rate: 17.71 births/1,000 population

Death rate: 4.31 deaths/1,000 population

Infant mortality rate: 9.01 deaths/1,000 live births

Life expectancy at birth:
total population: 77.4 years
male: 74.79 years
female: 80.14 years

Total fertility rate: 2.17 children born per woman

Religions: 76.3 percent Roman Catholic; approximately 14 percent Evangelical Protestant; others 10.3 percent

Languages: Spanish (official), English spoken around Puerto Limón

Literacy: 96 percent (2007 est.)

*All figures 2008 estimates, unless otherwise noted. Source: CIA World Factbook 2008.

of race, income level, or gender. Despite their faith in this ideal, however, the fact remains that some social and economic patterns form barriers.

The Power of the Well Born

A small number of families descended from the original *hidalgos* (Spanish nobles) have created a "dynasty of *conquistadores* (conquerors)," as Costa Ricans call it, for almost four centuries. Three of these families have produced 36 of Costa Rica's 49 presidents, and three-quarters of the congressmen during 1821–1970 could trace their ancestry to colonial overlords. Today, Costa Rican society disapproves of class differences, so presidents mix casually in public at festivals and parades, for example, often being addressed by their first names.

Still, wealth in Costa Rica clusters at the top of the social scale. The richest one percent of families receive 10 percent of the national income; the poorest 50 percent receive only 20 percent; and at least one-fifth of the population remain *marginados*—so poor they remain on the edges of mainstream society. Travelers to the countryside see that many farm families still live in simple huts. On the riverbanks of San José, shacks made of materials from the city dump—sheet metal, tires, oil barrels—create *tugurios*, or illegal shelters, for the poorest workers and their families. Still, most Costa Ricans try to keep up the appearance of being middle class by paying attention to the neatness of their homes and dress.

Those Who are not Mestizo

Costa Rica's approximately 125,877 blacks are the nation's largest minority. Most are descended from Jamaicans hired to build the Atlantic Railroad between San José and Puerto Limón in the late 19th century. At first, blacks were denied citizenship and the right to own land. During the late 1940s, impoverished black laborers of the United Fruit Company joined forces with Don Pepe Figueres in the 1948 Civil War. The 1949 constitution rewarded them by ending *apartheid* and guaranteeing blacks full citizenship. Today, many are better educated on average than their fellow countrymen and can be found in professions throughout the nation.

Native Americans have not fared as well in Costa Rica. Forced to flee from Spanish slavers into the mountains, most tribes broke into isolated groups. Today, in the remote valley forests of southern Costa Rica, about 9,000 Indians live where their ancestors once hid. Only the Chorotegas gradually became part of the national culture. The Borucas, who live in scattered villages in the Pacific southwest, have succeeded the best at preserving their old ways, including speaking their own language, sharing land, weaving traditional goods, and living under a *matriarchy*, or female-led society. Most Indians speak Spanish and practice versions of Catholicism.

There are 22 Indian reserves for eight different Indian tribes. In 1939, the government granted every Native American

Did You Know?

- In Costa Rica, there are three branches of government:
  Executive—president and two vice presidents, plus advisors
  Legislative—57 deputies
  Judicial—22 magistrates on the Supreme Court
- President and deputies are elected by popular vote to a four-year term. Supreme Court justices are elected for eight-year terms by the Legislative Assembly.
- Political candidates generally belong to one of two major parties: the National Liberation Party and the Social Christian Unity Party. However, there are several lesser parties active in politics and elections.
- The voting age is 18.

family farmland, and in 1977 it passed a law prohibiting the selling, leasing, or renting of land inside the reserves. Nevertheless, mining companies, hotel developers, and banana growers have been some of the culprits who have trespassed on Indian land in recent years. Because most Indians suffer from poverty-related illnesses, such as alcoholism, they are targets for *exploitation*.

Native children play near a cart in Tiquicia.

Over the years, immigrants have arrived in Costa Rica. Germans have succeeded for generations as coffee growers; Italians have settled in the town of San Vito on the central Pacific coast; several hundred **Quakers** live as a community around Monteverde; and thousands of refugees from Central American civil wars fled to Costa Rica and found work on the plantations. Chinese laborers, hired to work on the Atlantic Railroad, became the ancestors of many hotel, restaurant, and bar owners in Costa Rica, or businesspeople in the banana and cacao (chocolate) trade.

Costa Rican Men and Women

Gender roles in Costa Rica tend to be tied to traditional Catholic teachings about what men and women should do at home and in public. The cornerstone of society is still the family. Many households operate with the husband holding a higher rank in the relationship because he is the wage earner. Most wives raise the children and take care of the home.

Most younger Costa Ricans have abandoned the older ways of courtship, marriage, and behavior. Dating has replaced the *retreta*—men and women strolling together the central plaza—in even the smallest villages. Chaperoning, which calls for an adult accompanying a single young woman during a visit with a man, has disappeared. Short-term relationships are acceptable. In cities, unmarried couples living together is common. *Compañeras*, women in unmarried relationships, enjoy the same legal rights as wives. In the workplace, the law forbids sexual discrimination in hiring and salaries, and women are entitled to maternity leave and related benefits.

Professional women have enjoyed considerable success. Women outnumber men in many occupations, especially on university faculties. The nation's vice president from 1986–90 was a woman, Victoria Garrón de Doryan. That said, low-level jobs everywhere tend to be filled primarily by women. Also, Costa Ricans accept that men will father children with unmarried women. One-quarter of all children are *hijos naturales* (born out of wedlock); and one in five households is headed by a single mother.

Catholicism, the Official Religion

About 76.5 percent of Costa Ricans identify themselves as Catholic. Catholicism is the official state religion, and the government helps maintain churches and pays the salaries of bishops. Every village has a church and its own saints' day; religious icons dangle from the rearview mirrors of taxis and buses; and the Catholic marriage ceremony is the only one recognized by the state. Praying to a favorite saint is common, though Costa Ricans also enjoy keeping alive the folklore surrounding the power of witchcraft. The city of Escazú, it is said, is known for its *brujos*, witches who specialize in casting-out spells and fixing love problems.

Protestantism attracts fewer people, despite efforts by Protestant sects to win **converts** in Central and South America. Costa Rica's black population makes up about half of Costa Rica's approximately 604,212 Protestants.

More Teachers Than Soldiers

In 1869, Costa Rica became one of the first countries in the world to offer free public education to its people. Today, education is still held in high regard. "We have more teachers than soldiers," is a common boast. Schooling is required until age 14. Framed school diplomas hang in homes, even those located in tiny villages. Ninety-six percent of people ages 15 and older can read and write.

Since the 1970s, the country has invested more than a quarter of the national budget on education, but problems still remain. There is a shortage of good teachers; better-educated teachers are needed; and village libraries are the only way for many people to continue their education beyond elementary school. Many wealthy families send their children to private schools.

A popular form of education in Costa Rica is teaching Spanish to foreigners. Costa Rica's rich tradition in correct Spanish attracts visitors, who arrive for lessons. Missionaries of many faiths also come to Costa Rica to learn Spanish before locating in Spanish-speaking countries. Currently, there are 25 Spanish-language schools offering courses that can last a few days to a year or more.

(Opposite) This rodeo is part of a festival parade in Quebrada Grande, Guanacaste. The people of Costa Rica have many festivals and celebrations throughout the year. (Right) A Costa Rican craftsman carefully painting the wheel of a decorative oxcart. Costa Rica is known for its craftworkers.

5 Communities and Celebrations

IN COSTA RICA, there are plenty of museums, theaters, cinemas, festivals, and parades. On the other hand, there are not many artistic styles that can be found *only* in Costa Rica. Most can be traced to Spanish colonial days or have been borrowed from other Western cultures. With a Native American population of just one percent, Costa Rican arts and crafts tend to be a blend of modern popular tastes.

San José's famous Jade Museum amazes visitors with its colorful jade collection and many archaeological findings. The Gold Museum has Costa Rica's prized collection of ancient Indian gold, the kind that dazzled Columbus when he arrived in 1502. Moreover, the performing arts, such as dance and music, are flourishing. The National Symphony is highly regarded, and the 100-year-old National Theater stages some of the best dramatic productions in Central America.

Visitors who prefer the hustle and bustle of street parades and sidewalk cafes have many of those to choose from, too. Inexpensive eating places are called *sodas*. Dishes tend to be spiced and rely heavily on rice and beans, often accompanied by beef or chicken. No one dining in Costa Rica should turn down the opportunity to taste the coffee, which rates as some of the best in the world.

Arts and Crafts

Santa Ana and neighboring Escazú have long been havens for artists. In the 1920s, artists working in Escazú developed the distinctive Landscape Movement, which expressed a side of Costa Rica's personality in scenes of small villages set against a background of volcanoes. After a period of abstract painting in the 1950s, Costa Rican artists moved into a style that is known as "magical realism." Isidro Con Wong, from Puntarenas, is known for this style, with works in permanent collections in several United States and French museums. Formerly a poor farmer of Mongolian descent, he started painting with his fingers and *achiote*, a red paste made from a seed.

Some native crafts are still made in Costa Rica. The town of Guaitil retains the Chorotega Indian tradition of pottery. The Boruca Indians carve balsa-wood masks of supernatural beings. Santa Ana is also famous for its ceramics—large greenware bowls, urns, vases, coffee mugs, and small *adobe* houses fired in brick kilns and clay pits on the patios of family workshops.

Many of the best crafts in Costa Rica come from Sarchí. Visitors are welcome to enter the workshops and watch the families and master artists at work producing exquisitely curved bowls, serving dishes, and miniature versions of oxcarts, for which the village is known. The carts are painted in bright white or burning orange and are decorated with geometric designs and floral patterns. The women of Drake Bay are famous for *molas*, colorful and decorative hand-sewn appliqué used for blouses, dresses, and wall hangings.

The Centro Creativo, opened in 1991 in Santa Ana, west of Escazú, offers courses and studio space for local and visiting artists. The government-supported House of Arts in San José offers free lessons in painting and sculpture, and the Ministry of Culture holds exhibits on Sundays in city parks. University art galleries and the many smaller galleries scattered throughout San José exhibit works of all kinds.

Costa Rican Writing

Though the government, private **donors**, and the leading newspaper, *La Nacion*, sponsor literature through annual prizes, only a handful of writers make a living from writing in Costa Rica. Many of the stories and novels published use settings and situations that appeal mainly to Costa Ricans, but not much to the world beyond. Perhaps because the nation underwent a rather peaceful journey from colonialism to democracy, the literature is usually light—not about social clashes, struggles, or searches for identity. An outstanding exception is Julieta Pinto's *El Eco de los Pasos*, a novel about the 1948 Civil War.

Music, Dance, and Drama

Many dances, and much of the music of Costa Rica, have Indian and African roots, as well as Spanish. African-derived *marimba* (xylophone) music of Costa Rica is heard alongside the guitar, a popular instrument, especially as an accompaniment to folk dances, such as the Punto Guanacaste, a stomping dance for couples. This has been officially decreed as the national dance.

The heartland of traditional Indian music and dancing is the province of Guanacaste. Here, instruments used before Columbus' arrival, such as the *chirimia* (oboe) and *quijongo* (a single-string bow with gourd resonator), are still used for Chorotega tribal dances. In addition, the Borucas still perform their *Danza de los Diablitos*, and the Talamancas their *Danza de los Huelos*. Spanish-influenced dances are usually about enchanted lovers. They are based on the Spanish *paseo*, with women in white blouses and colorful skirts circled by men in white suits and cowboy hats.

A number of folkloric dance troupes tour the country, while others appear year-round at the Melico Salazar Theater, the Aduana Theater, and the National Dance Workshop headquarters in San José.

On the Caribbean coast, music is Afro-Caribbean in spirit and rhythm. Drums and banjos accompany a dance in which each dancer holds one of many brightly colored ribbons tied to the top of a pole. As they dance, they braid the ribbons. Visitors can hear calypso and reggae, too, both of which are played throughout the Caribbean.

In the larger cities, such as San José, dancers move to the rhythms of all sorts of music with Mexican, Central American, and South American origins—*cumbia, lambada, marcado, merengue, salsa, soca,* and Costa Rican swing music. Dance halls in small villages feature identical scenes of dancing couples on weekends. Costa Ricans listen and dance to North American popular music, too.

The Teatro Nacional (National Theater) is located in San José. The 100-year-old theater puts on some of the best dramatic productions in Central America.

Classical music in Costa Rica received a big boost with the formation of the National Symphony Orchestra in 1970. The orchestra, which performs in the National Theater, often features world-renowned guest soloists and conductors. Its season is April through November, with concerts on Thursday and Friday evenings, as well as Saturday matinees. Costa Rica holds an International Festival of Music during the last two weeks of August.

Costa Rica is said to have more theater companies per person than most countries in the world. The streets of San José are lined with tiny theaters, featuring comedy, drama, theater-in-the-round, mime, and even puppet theater. Crowds flock to these performances Tuesday through Sunday. Most performances are in Spanish, although some shows are performed in English. The English-speaking Little Theater Group is Costa Rica's oldest theatrical troupe. Theaters rarely hold more than 100 to 200 people and often sell out early.

Holiday Celebrations

Christmas in Costa Rica is a time for celebration and worship. In late November, decorations begin to appear in downtown shops. *Posadas* take place during the nine days before Christmas. Originating in Spain and Mexico, the *posada* is neighbors getting together each day to act out the pilgrimage of Joseph and Mary to Bethlehem. This is accompanied by singing and praying and lots of homemade *tamales*. Other traditional foods of the season include *pupusa* (a tortilla with cheese and corn); *vigorón* (cabbage, tomato, yucca, and fried pork rind served on a plantain leaf), and grilled pork, chicken, and sausage.

The traditional Christmas tree in Costa Rica is a big evergreen branch, a small cypress tree, or dried coffee branches. A popular Latin American tradition in Costa Rican homes is the *portal*, or a **nativity** scene, representing the birth of Jesus in the manger. The figure of baby Jesus is placed in the *portal* at midnight on December 24. That is also when the adults open their gifts. Thanks to the Costa Rican government, every worker in the country has extra money in December to spend on gifts. The Misa de Gallo, or Christmas Mass, takes place at midnight on December 24.

Parades, carnivals, parties, and religious processions take place throughout the country all during December, including the *tope*. In colonial times, the *tope* was used to select bulls for bullfights, but now it has become a formal parade of horses and gaily dressed riders down the main streets of San José. For many Costa Ricans, this parade is the biggest party event of the year. Bullfights are still held, too, but they are unique. Dozens of young men tease a bull in a ring, trying to get it to charge, which it often does!

The week before Easter Sunday is also a time for vacations throughout the country. Many businesses close the entire week. In most villages, towns, and cities, reenactments of Christ's crucifixion take place with actors in costume portraying biblical characters.

In the past, Costa Ricans used to celebrate Columbus Day in October. In recent years, however, it has been replaced by Día de la Raza—Race Day, a celebration of the human race as well as of Columbus' voyages.

Recognizing the strong influence by the Indians, Europeans, Africans, and Asians who have settled and lived here throughout its history, the purpose of another festival, Día de las Culturas (Culture Day) is to commemorate the invaluable contributions to this culture that is uniquely Costa Rican.

Did You Know?

These are the official holidays in Costa Rica. Other occasions are celebrated with parties and carnivals or family get-togethers. In addition, many towns hold a *festejo*, or festival, to honor its patron saint.

- January 1 – New Year's Day
- March/April – Holy Week
- April 11 – Juan Santamaría Day
- May 1 – Labor Day
- July 25 – Annexation of Guanacaste
- August 15 – Mother's Day
- September 15 – Independence Day
- October 12 – Day of the Cultures (Columbus Day)
- November 2 – All Souls' Day
- December 25 – Christmas

A Calendar of Costa Rican Festivals

Catholicism is the main religious denomination in Costa Rica, and celebrations reflect that fact. Whether celebrating a patron saint's day or a national holiday, however, Costa Rica's fiestas usually feature lots of food, music, rides, topes (horse parades), and bullfights (the bull is teased, but not harmed).

January

During the first two weeks of January, the **Palmares Fiestas** features folk dances, carnivals, music, rides, and bullfighting.

In the week of January 15, **Alajuelita Fiestas** are held to honor the Black Christ of Esquipulas, Alajuelita's patron saint, with an oxcart procession to a huge iron cross on the mountainside.

Santa Cruz Fiestas, held the week of January 15, feature folk dancing and bullfighting.

February

During the first week of February, **San Isidro de El General Fiestas** features cattle exhibits, agricultural and industrial fairs, bullfights, and flower exhibitions.

In late February, the Indian village of Rey Curre holds the **Fiesta of the Diablitos**. A fight is staged between Indians (diablitos) and the Spanish (a bull) in which colorful wooden masks and costumes create the scene.

March

The festival of **Dia de los Boyeros** (Oxcart Driver's Day) is held on the second Sunday of March. A parade of oxcarts is followed by competitions and the blessing of the animals and crops by local priests.

The **National Orchid Show** is held in mid-March. More than 500 local and foreign species and hybrids are on display.

On March 19, all neighborhoods named San Jose celebrate the **Saint Joseph's (San José) Day**. Religious celebrations are held with fairs and special Masses.

April

Holy Week—the week leading up to **Easter Sunday**—can fall either in March or April. Huge processions and festivals are held in all parts of the country during Easter week.

On April 11, **Juan Santamaría Day** commemorates Costa Rica's national hero, the barefoot soldier who gave his life in the battle with William Walker's troops in 1856. Week-long celebrations with marching bands, parades, concerts, and dances.

May

May 1: **Labor Day**
May 17: **Carrera de San Juan (San Juan Day)**

June

June 29: **Saints Peter & Paul Day**

July

On the Saturday closest to July 16, the **Virgin of the Sea** festival is held in Puntarenas.

Celebrations include colorful regattas of decorated fishing boats and yachts in the Nicoya Gulf carrying the town's patron saint, the Virgin of Mt. Carmel, along with parades, concerts, dances, sporting events, and fireworks.

July 25: **Guanacaste Day** celebrates the annexation of the province of Guanacaste from Nicaragua in 1824 with fiestas, folk dances, topes, cattle shows, bullfights, and concerts.

August

August 2: In Cartago, the festival of the **Virgin of Los Angeles** honors Costa Rica's patron saint, La Negrita, with a nationwide pilgrimage and religious processions to the Basilica in Cartago.

August 30: **San Ramón Day** features a religious procession of 30 saints from neighboring towns who come to visit San Ramón, the saint after whom the town is named. A person dressed as San Ramón goes dancing through the streets.

September

September 15: **Independence Day**.

October

October 12: **Columbus Day** is celebrated in the port city of Puerto Limón with week-long street dances, parades, and concerts.

October 12: Trés Rios celebrates its patron saint on **Virgen del Pilar's Day** with a parade and costumes made entirely of corn husks, grain, and silks.

November

November 2: **All Souls' Day**. The Day of the Dead is observed with family visits to graves of loved ones.

December

Nationwide Christmas celebrations begin in early December. Homes and businesses put up *portales* (nativity scenes). Competition for the best *portale* runs through December 22. Seasonal foods include coconut *melcochas* (candy), *chicha* (a drink made from corn), *tamales*, *rompope* (egg-nog), and imported apples and grapes.

During the week of December 8, the **Fiesta de los Negritos** is held in the Indian village of Boruca. An ancient Indian ritual is combined with honoring the Virgin of the Immaculate Conception. Extravagant costumes, music, and dancing are included.

Beginning December 15, carolers go from house to house and are treated to refreshments. At midnight on December 24, Catholic churches celebrate the **Misa de Gallo** (literally, Mass of the Rooster).

Festejos Populares (year end festivals) are celebrated in Zapote December 25–31. The fairground is transformed into an amusement park with lots of rides, food, bullfights, and fireworks.

December 26: **San Jose Tope**. A giant parade of horses takes place in downtown San Jose. The next day is the start of the San Jose Carnival, which features a parade of floats with music.

51

Recipes

Cartago Corn Cake

(Serves 6 to 8)
3/4 cup canned corn
1 stick (1/2 cup) unsalted butter, softened
1/2 cup sugar
1/4 cup plain yogurt
1 tsp. vanilla
2 tsp. freshly grated orange zest
3 large eggs
1 cup all-purpose flour
1/4 tsp. salt

Directions:

1. Preheat oven to 350 degrees F.
2. Butter 8 1/2"x 4 1/2" x 2 1/2" loaf pan.
3. Cut 3/4 cup of corn from cobs using a sharp knife.
4. Coarsely grind corn in food processor or blender, then drain in a sieve, pressing liquid from corn with back of spoon and discarding liquid.
5. Beat butter and sugar together in electric mixer bowl until light and fluffy.
6. Add yogurt, vanilla, and zest, and beat until smooth in same mixer bowl until combined.
7. Add one egg at a time, beating after each addition until combined.
8. Beat in corn, and add flour and salt, beating until just combined.
9. Spread batter evenly in pan, and bake in middle of oven for one hour or until golden (cake will not rise).
10. Cool cake in pan on a rack.

Black Beans, Hearts of Palm, and Corn Salad

(Serves 4)
1 16-oz. can black beans, rinsed and drained
1 10-oz. package frozen corn, thawed and drained
1 15-oz. jar of hearts of palm, drained and cut into 1/4-inch-thick rounds
2 large tomatoes, seeded and diced
1/2 red onion, minced
1/2 cup chopped fresh cilantro
1/4 cup olive oil
3 Tbsp. fresh lime juice
1 tsp. ground coriander

Directions:

Mix all ingredients in medium bowl. Season salad to taste with salt and pepper. (Salad can be prepared one day ahead). Cover and refrigerate.

Salsa

3 large ripe tomatoes, boiled or roasted, peeled, and cored
1 onion, chopped
3 serrano chiles, chopped
1 large clove garlic, sliced
2 Tbsp. extra-virgin olive oil
Salt

Directions

1. Roughly chop tomatoes in food processor or blender. Add onion, chiles, and garlic, and blend.
2. Heat oil in large skillet over medium heat. When hot, add salsa, and cook until it thickens slightly and returns to orange or red color—about 5 minutes. Add salt to taste, and set aside.

Tortillas and Eggs:

(Serves 6 to 8)
1/2 cup extra-virgin olive oil
1/2 14.8-oz. jar or can of hearts of palm, drained and diced
1 medium onion, coarsely chopped
1 medium clove garlic, chopped
1 dozen thin corn tortillas
1 dozen eggs, beaten
Salt
2 Tbsp. cilantro
1/4 cup plain yogurt thinned with 2 Tbsp. milk

Directions

1. Heat 2 Tbsp. oil in large skillet over medium heat. When hot, add onion and garlic, and cook until soft, about 5 minutes. Remove from heat, and set aside.
2. Wipe skillet clean with paper towel, and heat 1/3 cup oil over medium heat. Fry broken tortilla pieces in batches until lightly golden but not brown—3 to 5 minutes. Drain on paper towels.
3. Remove all but 2 tablespoons oil from skillet. Return to heat, add tortilla chips, and lightly toss in hot oil. Add eggs, salt to taste, onion, and garlic, and cook, stirring, until eggs are firm but moist, about 5 minutes. Add salsa, and lightly toss.
4. Transfer to platter. Drizzle with yogurt. Sprinkle on cilantro.

Mega Maca Muffins

(Makes 24 muffins)
2 1/4 cups cake flour
2 cups all-purpose flour
2 Tbsp. baking powder
1 1/4 cups sugar
3/4 tsp. salt
3/4 cup plus 1 tablespoon shortening
2 eggs
2 cups milk
1 teaspoon vanilla
1 cup chopped macadamia nuts
1 –8-oz. jar of pineapple jam

Directions:

1. Preheat the oven to 375 degrees.
2. Sift together cake and all-purpose flours, baking powder, sugar, and salt in bowl of electric mixer. Add shortening, and mix at medium speed using paddle attachment until the mixture is the texture of cornmeal.
3. In bowl, combine eggs, milk, and vanilla. Add to flour mixture. Mix until smooth, but do not overmix.
4. Grease muffin pans, and fill 2/3 full with muffin mixture. Sprinkle macadamia nuts over batter, and bake at 375 degrees F for 25 to 30 minutes, turning pans after 15 minutes to ensure even baking. When done, wood pick inserted near center of muffin will come out clean.

Glossary

Adobe—made from mud.

Aqueduct—an artificial channel used for bringing water from a distance.

Apartheid—racial separation, usually enforced by law.

Archipelago—a group of many islands.

Causeway—a raised road or path across shallow water.

Converts—people who change from one belief or faith to another.

Donor—a person who freely contributes money.

Economy—a system of producing, distributing, and using goods and services.

Eco-tourism—Responsible travel that contributes to conserving natural environments and puts money into the hands of the local people.

Ethics—standards of right and wrong.

Exploitation—taking advantage of; using unfairly.

Fauna—animals in a certain area.

Flora—plants in a certain area.

Geothermal—energy produced utilizing the heat of the Earth's interior.

Hydroelectric—electricity produced by water power.

Inflation—a sudden and sharp rise in prices.

Investment—money used to finance a business.

Labor Force—the work force of a country.

Matriarchy—a form of social order where women are in charge and are recognized as the heads of families, with power, lineage, and inheritance passing, where possible, from mothers to daughters.

Mercenaries—hired soldiers who serve in a foreign army.

Microclimate—the climate of a small area, such as a forest or valley.

Nativity—the birth of Jesus Christ.

Progressive—favoring improvement in government or society.

Quakers—the Religious Society of Friends, a Christian religious group.

Richter scale—a scale used for measuring the strength of earthquakes.

Seismologist—an expert in the study of earthquakes and shifts in the earth's crust.

Semi-nomadic—partly wandering or moving around.

Service industry—any business, organization, or profession that provides services instead of goods.

Tectonic—having to do with the structure of the earth's crust.

Tremor—a shaking or trembling.

Project and Report Ideas

Create a topographical map of Costa Rica's *cordilleras*, or mountain ranges— Guanacaste and Tilaran in the north, Central and Talamanca in the south.

Using a heavy piece of cardboard or poster board, first draw a large map of Costa Rica. Then, using a mixture of flour and paste, create three-dimensional mountain ranges. Refer to a topographical map that appears in an encyclopedia as a guide. Use watercolors to paint the mountain ranges when you're finished—be sure to label the ranges.

Create a "biography map" of Costa Rica.

Draw a large map of Costa Rica. Leave room in the margins to write paragraph biographies of these key figures in Costa Rican history:

Christopher Columbus	Juan Vasquez de Coronado	William Walker
Dr. Rafael Angel Calderón Guardia	General Tomás Guardia	Minor Keith
José María (Don Pepe) Figueres Ferrer	José María Figueres-Olsen	Juan Santamaría

Create an "ecology map" of Costa Rica.

Draw a large map of Costa Rica. Leave room in the margins to write one-paragraph descriptions of jungle or forest animals that live in Costa Rica.

Flashcards

Using the glossary in this book, create flashcards. Put the term on one side and the definition on the other. Practice with the cards in pairs. Then, choose two teams of three. Select a referee to say the term out loud, and then call on someone to give the definition. The referee's decision is final. Award points for each correct answer. You can also read the definition, and ask for the correct term instead!

Crafts

• Draw and write the front page of an imaginary newspaper proclaiming the victory of the Costa Ricans over William Walker's soldiers in April 1856. Don't forget to include the story of Juan Santamaría.

• In a travel guide, find examples of popular Costa Rican pottery bowls. Make papier maché bowls using newspaper and flour paste and building them over Styrofoam bowls. After the bowls have dried, paint them with acrylic paint in imitation of actual Costa Rican pottery. Spray the finished bowls lightly with a plastic coating.

Cross-Curricular Reports

• In teams, assemble a list of the best Web sites for finding out about Costa Rica. Devise a rating system. Include a one- or two-sentence summary about the site. Combine these sites into a comprehensive guide to Costa Rica on the Internet for other classes to use.

• Find an example of one type of Costa Rican music. Play it for the class and explain it in your report.

• Write one-page, five-paragraph reports answering any of the following questions. Begin with a paragraph of introduction, then three paragraphs each developing one main idea, followed by a conclusion that summarizes your topic:

What is the relationship between tectonic plates, earthquakes, and volcanoes?

What elements create a microclimate?

Why is coffee only grown in certain areas of the world?

Who created the Richter scale? How is it used?

Are all rainforests the same?

Would you rate Christopher Columbus as a successful explorer? Why or why not?

What are some examples of "eco-tourism"?

Explain, using diagrams, the difference between hydroelectric and geothermal energy.

How is chocolate made? How was it used in the Mayan civilization?

Who were the conquistadors? What was their mission?

Why was building the Atlantic Railroad in Costa Rica thought to be an impossible task?

What is "magical realism" in literature or painting?

10,000 B.C.	Indian communities dot the landscape of present-day Costa Rica.
A.D. 1400s	Chorotegas, or "fleeing people," arrive from southern Mexico, bringing with them a highly developed civilization.
1502	On September 8, Christopher Columbus lands near present-day Puerto Limón during his fourth voyage to the Caribbean. He calls the region La Huerta (The Garden).
1539	By now, the region is known to the Spanish as Costa Rica—"the rich coast."
1821	September 15, Costa Rica officially declares independence from Spain after Guatemala declares independence for all of Central America.
1856	During March and April, Costa Ricans repel an invading army sent by an American adventurer, William Walker.
1870–1882	General Tomás Guardia overthrows the government and institutes a number of forward-looking reforms.
1940–1944	Dr. Rafael Angel Calderón Guardia serves as president, leading a reform movement that favors the poor.
1948	When Calderón's party loses the election and he refuses to step aside, Jose Maria (Don Pepe) Figueres Ferrer leads a 40-day revolt that gives power to Calderón's opponent in the election.
1949	November 7, Costa Rican legislature ratifies the current constitution.
1953–1957	Figueres continues many of Calderón's reform policies and puts in place his own, including abolishing the military.

1983   Costa Rica issues a proclamation of neutrality in response to civil wars in Central America.

1987   President Oscar Arias Sánchez receives the Nobel Peace Prize for his efforts in leading five Central American presidents to sign his peace plan in Guatemala City.

1990s   Costa Rica embarks on programs designed to strengthen its economy, through such measures as retiring the national debt and encouraging the growth of high-tech industry.

1996   Hurricane César causes 41 deaths and $39 million in damages.

2000   The Costa Rican government offers free e-mail service in public places, and makes private Internet access rates cost approximately the same as in North America.

2002   Abel Pacheco is elected president of Costa Rica with 58 percent of the vote.

2004   In January, Costa Rica concludes negotiations with the United States to participate in the U.S.-Central America Free Trade Agreement.

2006   Oscar Arias Sánchez is re-elected president of Costa Rica.

2008   A report by the UN's International Labor Organization finds that Costa Rica has the lowest unemployment rate in all of Latin America and the Caribbean.

2010   In February, Laura Chinchilla becomes the first woman elected president of Costa Rica.

Further Reading/Internet Resources

Firestone, Matt, and Wendy Yanagihara. *Costa Rica*. Oakland, Calif.: Lonely Planet, 2008.

Foster, Lynn V. *A Brief History of Central America*. New York: Checkmark Books, 2007.

Helmuth, Chalene. *Culture and Customs of Costa Rica*. Westport, Conn.: Greenwood Press, 2000 .

Henderson, James D., et al, editors. *A Reference Guide to Latin American History*. Armonk, N.Y.: M.E. Sharpe, 2000.

Koutnik, Jane. *Costa Rica: A Quick Guide to Customs and Etiquette*. New York: Kuperard, 2006.

Travel information

http://www.centralamerica.com/cr/info/index.htm
http://www.redrival.com/cyclerica/portals/resources.htm

History and Geography

http://www.cocori.com/library/crinfo/juansa.htm
http://www.lonelyplanet.com/worldguide/costa-rica/

Economic and Political Information

https://www.cia.gov/library/publications/the-world-factbook/geos/cs.html
http://travel.state.gov/travel/cis_pa_tw/cis/cis_1093.html
http://www.loc.gov/rr/international/hispanic/costarica/costarica.html

Culture and Festivals

http://www.cocori.com/library/crinfo/xmasincr.htm
http://www.costaricabureau.com/cultural.htm

The official promotion and regulating agency for tourism is the Costa Rica Tourist Board (ICT). The Board's address is:

Instituto Costarricense de Turismo
Apartado 777-1000
San Jose, Costa Rica
Telephone: (506) 222-1090
          or 223-1733, ext. 277
Toll-free U.S. number: 1-800-327-7033
Fax: (506) 223-5452 or 555-4997
Web: http://www.visitcostarica.com

U.S. Department of Commerce
Trade Information Center
International Trade Administration
14th and Constitution Avenue NW
Washington, DC 20320
Telephone: 800-USA-TRADE
Website address: http://www.ita.doc.gov

Costa Rican American Chamber of Commerce
c/o Aerocasillas
P.O. Box 025216, Dept 1576
Miami, Florida 33102-5216
e-mail: chamber@amcham.co.cr
Web: http://www.amcham.co.cr

Public Affairs Office
Embassy of the United States
Apartado 920-1200 Pavas, San José, Costa Rica
Telephone: (506) 220-3939
Fax: (506) 232-7944
e-mail:hdssjo@pd.state.gov

Index

Contributors

Senior Consulting Editor **James D. Henderson** is professor of international studies at Coastal Carolina University. He is the author of *Conservative Thought in Twentieth Century Latin America: The Ideals of Laureano Gómez* (1988; Spanish edition *Las ideas de Laureano Gómez* published in 1985); *When Colombia Bled: A History of the Violence in Tolima* (1985; Spanish edition *Cuando Colombia se desangró, una historia de la Violencia en metrópoli y provincia*, 1984); and co-author of *A Reference Guide to Latin American History* (2000) and *Ten Notable Women of Latin America* (1978).

Mr. Henderson earned a bachelors degree in history from Centenary College of Louisiana, and a masters degree in history from the University of Arizona. He then spent three years in the Peace Corps, serving in Colombia, before earning his doctorate in Latin American history in 1972 at Texas Christian University.

Charles J. Shields, the author of all eight books in the Discovering Central America series, lives in Homewood, a suburb of Chicago, with his wife Guadalupe, an elementary-school principal. He has a degree in history from the University of Illinois in Urbana-Champaign, and was chairman of the English department and the guidance department at Homewood-Flossmoor High School in Flossmoor, Illinois.